Blockchain

———— ✂︎❧ ————

The Untapped Goldmine of Blockchain that Virtually No One Knows About

By reading this document, the reader agrees that under no circumstances is the author responsible for any losses, direct or indirect, which they may incur because of the use of information contained within this document, including, but not limited to, —errors, omissions, or inaccuracies.

Table of Contents

Introduction

You will see a new beginning in this book, "*Blockchain: The Untapped Goldmine of Blockchain that Virtually No One Knows About.*" While the world waits, the secrecy of the cryptocurrency deepens. The arrival of Blockchain as a new way forward has promised many things including an unveiling of new technologies, though sharing is the keyword here. The idea of being in touch with innovation is the lure for the scientists of the future. The average person remains puzzled because this is so new.

Many do not have the answer to the question, "Is Blockchain the beginning or the end?" Indeed, we have many more who are not waiting, for they do not believe in the future of mystical coins. They remain stuck in the mire of flat currency, though the future of paper and coin money may be that it doesn't have much use, but then they never really did.

Will we see a world where we talk money over the Internet? Is there a reality that promises equal sharing of information and systems? Happily, for us, this is coming true!

Introduction

The road to this mystical land of openly shared technologies has come through because of Blockchain. Read more about how this happened and learn how you can take part in it. The future awaits you and the better your understanding of it, the easier you will find the gradual transition.

Chapter 1:

The Emerging World of Decentralized Currency

T he early work on the chain of blocks that ultimately became Blockchain occurred due to the work of W. Scott Stornetta and Stuart Haber in 1991, who described the method of securing the blocks cryptographically. Ross J. Anderson, in 1996, and the duo of John Kesley and Bruce Schneier followed this work in 1998. In the same year, Nick Szabo worked on bit gold, the decentralized digital currency and its mechanism.

Solution to double spending

After two years, in the year 2000, Stefan Konst came forward with the solution that was set to help create these secured chains. The public announcement of the first Blockchain as a concept occurred in 2008. Satoshi Nakamoto implemented the concept as a core part of the bitcoin digital currency. The autonomous management of the public ledger through the peer-to-peer network and a server with distributed timestamping improved the functioning of the bitcoin currency. This, in effect, solved the "double spending" problem of all digital currencies. Since then, many other digital currencies have modeled themselves based on the bitcoin.

Issue the Blockchain addressed

When first used for the bitcoin, the Blockchain was used to serve the double purpose of having autonomy and possessing an inherently safe database. Moreover, by 2014, new applications came into being that were based on the "Blockchain" database that remained distributed on the Internet. On another level, implementation of the programmable Blockchain allowed users access to smart programs in programming languages that incorporated self-paying invoices when the shipment reached its destination. In the same way, one could visualize share certificates that paid owners the interest when the market value of the share reached a certain limit.

Increase in scope of Blockchain 2.0

Blockchain 2.0 technology was thus born to take the concept of digital currency beyond mere transactions and having an exchange value for money to removing the need for intermediaries with power to act as mediators for the information and the transaction. The scope of the currency will eventually help people shut off the financial world to enter and profit from sharing their information. This will make sure proper compensation for all intellectual property is established, since the identity of the person is secure.

Key features of Blockchain

These helps eliminate the problems of social inequality since people could store their personal information along with their digital ID. This changed the distribution pattern of the wealth. Here are the key features of the Blockchain.

1. You can make secure transactions online with Blockchain

2. You have two kinds of records in the Blockchain database

3. You can check different blocks separately

4. Blockchain is constantly being upgraded

Make secure transactions online

Blockchain is the protocol that allows you to exchange value online. This can include money, property, documents and even votes. You do this using Blockchain. The records oblige acceptance and offer because the Blockchain gives title rights. You can make a global record on thousands of computers globally. Once you do this, you cannot ever alter that digital record. Since the system exists in a decentralized state, anyone can see the records if they want to. This means there is nothing hidden and there is always proof that the transaction took place.

This also adds to the system safety though some feel skeptical over the data security. The vigorous workflow motivated by self-interest undergoes verification through collective teamwork. This type of protocol for the exchange of value is cheap, fast and always correct.

Two kinds of records

One can see a Blockchain as having a hash chain within another one. You see two records here – the hash chain record and the block it is linked to. We batch the valid transactions and put them into blocks. After this, we hash them and encode them as the Merkle tree. All the blocks in the Blockchain have links to each other in the order in which people made them.

Linking in this way ensures that all the blocks have integrity and one can trace them back to the original one where it all began.

Evaluate different blocks

Evaluation of the blocks occurs simultaneously though they do not bear any correlation to one another. This results in a fork that is soon resolved when the evaluation is complete. We use a specified algorithm to score different historical versions as this allows us to select one with a higher value. This is apart from the hash links one uses to connect to the earlier block.

Therefore, a look at the peers (original block) that support the database will enable users to see different historical versions. This they do, forgoing the highest scoring version at the time the choice is made. We refer to blocks that are not chosen as orphan blocks.

Value of the Blockchain is changing every moment

Blockchain creates new blocks sometimes as often as every 10 seconds. We say the Blockchains grow in height as they grow older. We split the Blockchains into layers for better management. As we add new blocks to the Blockchain, the value of the Blockchain increases or decreases, depending on the block added.

When peers receive a new version, they broaden and overwrite their existing database. Then, they send this new version to their peers. The new version is usually an old version with one new block added. One cannot say that any one version will remain the best all the time. This is due to the priority given to new work that adds to the score and not to the copying of the old work to make it into new work.

This increases the possibility that another entry will shortly supersede the new one. This way, as the block grows in height, the value will decrease exponentially. Another cause for determining the value is the proof-of-work method. Here, the block with the most number of proof-of-works becomes the most valued.

We may use any number of methods to test a Blockchain provided one has computational accuracy. Usually one adopts a redundant computational level and not the traditional parallel way where you have enough segregation. You can parse the Blockchain to get any information you need.

Concept of Decentralization

Blockchain stores the data across the network and not in any one central place. This kind of decentralization is a key aspect of the Blockchain network. Thus, there are none of the inherent drawbacks of the centrally controlled database system.

Public key cryptography is an essential part of the safety aspect of Blockchain. This public key refers to an address in the Blockchain through a randomly generated number string. When a person sends money, using a randomly generated public key, the network will record the transaction as belonging to that public key.

The private key is much like the public key in that you can use it to interact with others and exchange money and assets. However, the private key belongs to you alone. Everyone will have a private key and this forms the basis for the transaction.

Inside the network, every miner (or node) has access to the entire network. Trust is equal, meaning that everyone has the same amount of trust. Because of the enormous database replication, you stay assured of the data quality.

1. We do not keep a central copy of the data

2. Everyone has the same trust

3. Every transaction is broadcast throughout the network

4. We do the delivery of the message on a 'better quality' basis

5. All the nodes working at that time will record the transaction

6. We send this completed block to all the other nodes

Blockchain marks the changes using a timestamp method. One example of such is the proof-of-work while other methods include proof of burn and proof-of-stake.

Typical Workflow inside a Blockchain

1. Initiation of transaction after the person signs in digitally

2. One miner receives this transaction and he verifies it

3. This transaction becomes the block that is broadcast to the entire network

4. Network checks that the data is valid and then accepts it if it is right

5. We send the transaction to the receiver

Open and permissioned Blockchains

We had a few Blockchains some time back that had ownership records, which did not allow open access to viewing. You could view the Blockchain of course. Most of the Blockchains at that time were open Blockchains that did not need any permission for viewing. This gave rise to the controversy over the very definition of Blockchain. Users raised the question whether a private system with permissioned verifiers under a central authority should come under the Blockchain category.

The users who were for this form of system say that any time-stamped batches of data can become a Blockchain. Here, the system prevents the spending of the same single output and at the same time prevents modifying of a single object by two separate transactions in the Blockchain.

One sees parallels drawn to the corporate database and the permissioned Blockchain. While they both do not support decentralized data verification, they do not have a hard defense against tampering or operator tampering. One sees the need to alter the viewpoint of the Blockchain that is merely a distributed database or ledger. People began to debunk the permissioned system as nothing more than hot air.

Advantage of the permission less database

Since one does not need access control, we need not stand guard against malevolent forces. This great big advantage means that anyone could add any application on the network and not have to worry about seeking permissions and the like. They merely use the Blockchain as a transport module.

Disadvantages of the permissioned database

We encourage directness and group effort in the permissioned database network. However, due to the permission protocol, they will always restrict those who they do not want to transact within their network. This lack of transparency is clear and they have no network benefit either. This is because they do not use anonymous miners for confirming the user name in their transactions. They should woo the miners and many big corporations to use private Blockchain networks. One need not have a 51% controlling stake in the private network.

If one could attack the private database, one would control 100% of the network. You could then alter the private corporate server transactions in any way you wished. This could have very serious implications, especially during any financial crisis. Unlike the bitcoin, Blockchain, where gigawatts of computing power protected every transaction, the private Blockchains had no means to protect their network. Lastly, there is no need for race and compulsion to use more power to discover the blocks fast in the private Blockchains. These become just boring databases, which remain a burden to keep up.

Chapter 2:

A Fresh Perspective on Blockchain

The anonymous online ledger called Blockchain has no central authority, unlike the bank ledgers that come under central control. Thus, one could interact with a perfect stranger on the Internet and make a successful contract without the need for any third-party authorization. The two parties agreed on something they know is true. The distributed network that takes care of the genuineness of the transaction remains chained to each other through the cryptography signature. As mentioned before, the entry to the network could exist as open or permissioned. If everyone is pre-selected, then the network is permissioned. When the world can reach this process, we call it "open" or "un-permissioned."

The role of the banks

Banks have a never-ending need for ledgers and records of transactions. They need related back-end functions that help them meet the demands of their customers. With a decentralized ledger, everyone - including the banks - can update records, note transactions and make entries into their own block. Moreover, the ledger is permanent and we cannot erase or remove these entries. They can track documents and authenticate ownership just as easy as sending an email.

Extending this technology to land and deeds

The Honduras government has created a public ledger through Blockchain and put all land records on it. If someone was to sell a piece of land or buy some property, it comes onto the public records at once. Everyone sees the change in ownership instantly.

The Australian Securities Exchange (ASX) has plans to move its equity clearing and settlement system on to the Blockchain system. Last year, NASDAQ showed how it used the Blockchain-based technology, Linq, to represent digitally share ownership.

They preferred this technology to the traditional banks because they did not want any intermediary. The transactions were secure, as it were, since the records remained secure right across the Blockchain network.

The ledger remained tamper-proof and the system was transparent.

Types of Forks

When users at two different nodes in the Blockchain disagree on algorithms or protocol to follow, they both run their version of the Blockchain software. Here we see that two distinct Blockchains appear and their histories from that point onwards are separate. When they do this, they can agree to combine at some future point or they can agree to disagree.

When they agree to agree at some future point, they form a soft fork or the fork is forward compatible. If they do not want to see any other point of view, they can opt for the hard fork.

Applications for Blockchain

The biggest benefit one hopes to see is the expansion in the number of customers and merchants who use Blockchain. This would open the market towards a rapid cashless society with everything transparent to everyone. However, this does not happen at present.

Merchants, for instance, do not want to take too much risk by using the cryptocurrencies at the core of their businesses. Obviously, the crypto currency remains the main application emerging from the Blockchain scenario.

- Cryptocurrencies – bitcoin, BlackCoin, Nxt, Dash

- Distributed cloud – Storj

- Distributed registry – Factom

- Decentralized applications – MaidSafe

- Decentralized messaging – Gems

- Decentralized exchanges

- Digital identity

- Communication enhancement in the supply chain

- Digital voting and forums

- Smart contracts

- Notary service

- Fair trade music

- Prediction market

- Boardroom

- IOT

- Health

- Government

- Law and Contract

- Finance and banking

On a broader note, the Republic of Georgia has initiated a property registry using Blockchain. Moreover, one can see the effectiveness and speed of transactions of land deals at Sweden Land Registry.

There is little wonder, therefore, that the insurance companies find the thing exciting and lucrative. One of the reasons is that we have new distribution methods once they adopted the Blockchain method. This would include parametric insurance, peer-to-peer insurance along with micro-insurance. Banks get the benefit since the systems for back office settlements will speed up.

The other application that would benefit is online voting. This would make sure of a bigger participation from the public. Systems that share many collaborating peers such as the IoT will benefit from Blockchain. Another system in this group would consist of the information database for medical records. To that end, we see making books and text into digital form will make retrieval and sharing of print media easy.

Birth of smart contracts

Use of smart contracts obviates the need for detailed follow-up. This is because the smart contract will pay and deduct the money as and when needed. Every smart contract will automatically put an escrow into place. For one, the IMF is for the use of Blockchains, as this will cut the moral hazards due to less paperwork, thereby making the contracts more workable. However, the legal standing should clarify itself only as time passes.

One could set a smart contract to begin executing when the contractors meet some set of conditions. Thus, these programming instructions could define, execute and even mediate changes when needed. The scope of such contracts is limitless but one must set a minimum standard that will make a contract qualify as a smart contract. As of now, none of the cryptocurrencies uses a smart contract system.

Need for a centralized cryptocurrency

People tend to reject technology if they think that someone else had the first try. For this reason, when we introduce any centralized online currency, we must make sure that everyone gets it at the same time. Selected central banks in a few countries such as Singapore, United States, England, Sweden, China and South Africa have plans to issue the Central Bank

Issued Cryptocurrency (CICC) but none has taken any concrete steps yet.

Creation of alternate Blockchains

This is an automatic reaction to the existing Blockchain scenario. Alternate Blockchains or Altchains are all the databases that use Blockchain technology but are not part of the main Blockchain. They use Blockchain coding and work in the same way as the real Blockchain.

The idea behind such Altchains is to improve the functionality. For example, one could use an Altchain to use their book database in schools. Operating facility for using bitcoins is another advantage for the Altchains. Thus, Altchains will have better anonymity, storage, applications (smart contract) and high performance. This extension of the Blockchain will help to end another intermediary and increase the reach over the Internet to things that matter - especially finance.

Impact of Altchains

Here are a few prominent examples of non-cryptocurrency applications:

- ***Steemit***: This is a joint cryptocurrency and networking site. You can blog and meet people and exchange currency.

- ***Bitnation***: The Blockchain powers this jurisdiction. This operating nation is the first Decentralized Borderless Voluntary Nation.

- ***Hyperledger***: This is an effort at collaborating across various segments of the industry to support distributed ledgers. These ledgers have their basis on the Blockchain.

- ***Synereo***: Communication based on Blockchain that support synchronous and asynchronous communications.

- ***Bitcache***

- ***DECENT Network***: This is the platform for content distribution.

- ***Swarm and Koinify***: These crowdfunding sources remain decentralized using Blockchain.

- **_Counterparty_**: This open source platform for finance allows one to create financial applications on a peer-to-peer basis. Again, the Blockchain supports the entire thing.

- **_LaZooz_**: This decentralized site allows you share rides in real-time.

The simplest step forward for the Blockchain technology now is to bring into force copyright registration. Then, the public ledger system becomes permanent and transparent for everyone to compile data on any public interactive event (such as sales). If everyone adopted this universally, one could copyright his or her music videos, their real-time videos, and anything else they wished.

More importantly, one could track the sales through a network using Blockchain and know the status without having to ask. The smart technology would give him or her the information the moment they logged into the system.

Involvement of top organizations

Many commercial organizations revealed plans about their future that involved Blockchain and the use of distributed ledgers. Here are some of them:

1. ***Microsoft Visual Studio***: Application developers can now access the Solidity language of Ethereum.

2. ***Satoshi Citadel Industries***

3. ***Swiss Stock Exchange, Zurich Cantonal Bank*** and ***Swisscom***: This Swiss consortium uses Ethereum technology based on Blockchain to give over-the-counter asset trading.

4. ***R3 Company***: This Company helps connect 42 banks through Ethereum to distributed ledgers. The other collaborators include IBM, Monax.io, Chain.com, and Intel.

5. ***Digital Asset Holdings***: Its CEO Blythe Masters leads this.

6. ***SafeShare Insurance***: Lloyd's of London has underwritten this insurance of the sharing economy based on Blockchain approach.

7. ***Deloitte and ConsenSys***: They announced a plan to create a digital bank named Project ConsenSys.

8. ***Context Labs***: This concern develops platforms based on Blockchain.

Chapter 3:

Fundamentals of the IBM Blockchain

Blockchain technology represents one aspect of progress through disruptive innovation. It decreases friction between global businesses and enhances trust between the interacting parties.

Through its shared immutable ledger, Blockchain has ushered in a new era of technology where transparency, accountability and trust reigns supreme. With an effort to improve on the existing versions of Blockchain, IBM Blockchain has entered The Hyperledger Project. Until now, Blockchain had anonymous users with cryptocurrencies such as bitcoins operating in a public network. This new Blockchain for business will rely on permissioned users within the network. This eliminated the need for the use of cryptocurrencies.

Extending the use of Blockchain across the professions and industries

Great utility value of Blockchain for business applications

- Settlement of securities by financial institutions now could occur within a few hours. One had to wait for days for the transaction to come through.

- By sharing production logs with regulators and original equipment manufacturers, one could cut the number of product recalls.

- Commercial enterprises could organize their flow of goods and manage payments with lesser risk and higher speed. This could apply to various branches of the society including Healthcare, Government, Banking, and Finance. You could find it applicable in areas such as retail, manufacturing, legal, insurance, finance and accounting, supply chain and logistics, media and entertainment.

IBM is one of the premium members of the Hyperledger Project by the Linux Foundation. It has regulatory transparency and governance takes place openly. Moreover, it is open sourced and permissioned. The unique approach of

IBM takes into consideration the three pillars – Community, Cloud and Client.

Until now, IBM has contributed 44,400 lines of code to help advance the technology for distributed ledger and build the open source code. Thus, the Hyperledger Project is growing. On the cloud level, critical business aspects such as performance, security, compliance, high-availability and related value-added services remains available through IBM Bluemix. Lastly, IBM Blockchain experts from different parts of the globe begin a workshop experience for clients in a partnership; they help build and carry out independent Blockchain solutions.

Changes happen

When people first came across Blockchain and the Bitcoin, they had doubts. These were probably justified, for they needed some authority to tell them that the online ledger needed no change. One got the confidence through simpler implementations of the Blockchain such as for shopping or interacting in a social network to get the confidence in the permanence and security of the distributed ledger network. The growing community sustained this currency and so it grew. Nobody manipulated it and nobody has absolute control over the network.

One undeniable dimension of Blockchain was its dependence on the computational power of the miners in the Blockchain network. They provided the base for the existence and survival of the Blockchain network. In addition, they used electric power to make their computations, much more than in any ordinary household or office.

To this extent, one can compare the energy consumed by the Blockchain network as that consumed by a nation – Ireland to be exact. However, that is an exaggeration but it gives you an idea of the huge nature of the demand for power here. The transparent, permanent and independent database that the community shares and coexists in many locations at the same time we refer to as a mutual distributed ledger (MDL).

Change the way we do business

Blockchain is the way we record anything and that includes contracts, agreements and transactions into a digital ledger and verify the event as having occurred. Since we store the ledger in many places, spread across the Internet, anyone in the network can have access to the event as it happens right across the globe.

The exciting thing is when we realize that this transaction could extend to mean anything – bicycles, diamonds, dollars or anything else. All the transactions remain bunched into blocks and they are bound cryptographically. Then they are bound chronologically into the chain with complex mathematical algorithms.

This complex procedure makes it difficult, if not impossible, for a hacker to get hold of any one transaction. He or she would have to get all the copies in the network that has copies of the transaction and then change them simultaneously to do a successful hack.

By encryption, we mean that the transaction undergoes hashing. This occurs on many computers (hundreds sometimes) at one time. Moreover, they all must agree on the answer to do a successful hash.

We know the transaction is secure because we cannot convert the hash back to its original value. If we alter the original document, it would produce a different digital signature that updates the records on the network. Therefore, theoretically speaking fraud has a less likely chance of happening and if it does, we can spot it easily.

This has been the underlying concept that gave birth to the digital currency, Bitcoin. This happened in 2008 and required lots of computers, electricity and computing power. Bitcoin is the technology underpinning the solving of complex mathematical puzzles. In addition, many companies are developing their Blockchain services through permissioned or open networking. These include the big ones like Microsoft and Ethereum.

In the banks where we keep our money, a similar thing is taking place. The only thing is that, for the banks, the interactions are costly as the computers talk to each other over a huge network. Banks necessarily talk to each other and this keeps the financial system intact. However, because the system is getting old and the costs are rising, one sorely feels the need for a newer and cheaper method of 'talking' to help keep up the financial integrity.

Banks could start using intermediaries just as in the case of Blockchains and remove, at the same time, a lot of unnecessary regulations and processes. It would speed things up. This type of open ledger of transactions would make the accounting work easy. It could detect tax frauds and this has opened a completely new world of possibility.

The tech company, R3 CEV, has successfully persuaded banks and financial institutions to join in making the distributed ledger technology consortium. It involves banks such as Wells Fargo, Barclays and UBS among others. Recently it announced that 11 financial institutions had taken part in the token exchange experiment. This took place across the global private network. There was no verification by a third central party.

The meaning of this is clear. When the banks took the costs out of the system, increased the speed of the transactions, and brought every transaction to the common ledger, it would raise the effectiveness of the system. You could have fast systems for a lesser cost. You could send money abroad instantaneously.

This is extendable for almost anything. Therefore, it is no surprise that the tech company, Everledger, wants the miners to fall in with the Kimberley Process using the Blockchain. The Kimberley Process is the government regulation and community backed scheme that certifies that diamonds being mined were not used for the funding of terrorism.

Through this process, they make the record of the value of the diamonds along with its ownership history on the Blockchain system. Anyone who wants the information could reach it at any time. You cannot tamper with this information or change it in any way. So much so, during six months, Everledger added 850,000 diamonds to the records.

Another example of the way Blockchain is helping the digital revolution is the case of the tech firm, Guardtime. Based in Estonia, Guardtime is busy using Keyless Signature Infrastructure to manage the data of its citizens. They have a network that spreads across 1,000 services online. They protect the data and help organize the massive data.

Protection is on the top of the list and they have initiated real-time tamper detection to the critical infrastructure. Apart from that, they help global telecom companies such as Ericsson help to keep up the core integrity of their network. Being the era of the Internet of Things and using Big Data, they found it easy to add their digital signature to the data they had. This proved very useful. In addition, being able to add the digital signature to the stages of development will help to enhance reliability and quality. Though one may not understand the Blockchain technology too well, it does have a profound impact on all of us.

Blockchain Explorer

Blockchain-explorer aims to create user-friendly web applications. This project is in incubation. The Hyperledger will view or query transactions and associated data, blocks and any information stored in the ledger that it considered relevant. It could view and query network information such as name, status and a list of nodes, view, invoke, deploy and query chain codes and transaction families.

Hyperledger Fabric

The fabric consists of the use of the Blockchain technology intended to give Blockchain solutions and applications. This resulted from the first hackathon. At this point, a merger began between the proposal of DAH and that of IBM. Its modular architecture allows the users to plug-and-play the various components such as membership and consensus services. Through the application logic of the system called the chaincode, one could host smart contracts by leveraging container technology.

The fabric incubator has three repositories – fabric (Gerrit), fabric-api (Gerrit), and fabric-chaintool.

Hyperledger Iroha

The easy and simple to integrate distributed ledger projects for all infrastructural projects that needed the distributed ledger technology. The main features of Iroha are as follows:

- It has a simple construction.

- It has Sumeragi – a new chain based byzantine algorithm. This consensus algorithm is fault tolerant.

- The main thrust is on mobile application development.

- The design is modern and based on the domain-driven C++

Sawtooth Lake

This is a highly versatile and scalable modular Blockchain suite. It is modular Blockchain suite of Intel. The wide potential of distributed ledgers extends from Financials to IoT and so the needs will change across the field. One may use both permissioned and permission-less versions in the Sawtooth Lake. You can see the Proof of Time (PoET) algorithm, which is new. The PoET reduces the resources consumption to the least while targeting large distributed populations for validation. One may use restricted or unfettered semantics with the Transaction Families. These Transaction Families arise from the consensus layer after decoupling the Transaction Business Logic. The entire project exists in a single repository. Consolidation takes place for the multiple repositories that we had previously.

New Blockchain initiative by Swift

To increase global liquidity, the global financial messaging services provider, Swift, announced the launch of the Proof of Concept (PoC). This is to decide whether the Distributed Ledger Technology (DLT) or the Blockchain system will come in useful for the banks to improve the management of their Nostro databases.

Swift and Accenture had previously come together to build a platform. When the news of a hacking broke out, they concluded in their paper that Blockchain was not effective at keeping third parties out of trades. In this latest press release, they seem to have adopted Blockchain fully and made it part of the global payments innovation (gpi) initiative undertaken by Swift. This will help set up a new standard in cross-border payment. They roped in the leading correspondent banks to collaborate with the new PoC. They expect the member gpi Swift banks to take part. They begin in a few months.

The current models of correspondent banking need banks to watch funds in their overseas accounts. They could do this through end of the day statements and credit and debit card statements. This working and maintenance work constituted a major chunk of the cost-border payment costs. The PoC will run to decide the efficacy of the distributed ledger system in lowering operational risks and costs.

By deploying the Hyperledger technology, which was open-source, and combining it with Swift assets they hope to find a functioning method that suits the requirements of the financial industry. In this case, the private Blockchain along with specific user profiles and strong data control will come into place. They would govern the user privileges and data access strictly.

Chapter 4:

IBM brings Blockchain to Developers through the Cloud

IBM has moved Blockchain to the cloud putting it in direct access to the developers. This has open myriad possibilities since the Blockchain now has its own platform in the cloud. Since it has its basis on open-source technology, the possibilities for developing end-user friendly applications were endless. The Fabric is the first incubation project of the Hyperledger project by Linux Foundation. Now, Open Blockchain is a part of the Fabric.

IBM wants more developers to join in the collaborative project to create a Blockchain for business. Open Blockchain (OBC) will consist of transactions, which is the ledger of digital events. Every participant who has a stake in the event will have a share. You can never change the information once you have recorded it.

You can update the information only by consensus of the participants. This consensus is cryptographically verifiable and is in keeping with the agreement among the participants. Technically speaking, the fabric architecture OBC facilitates businesses to use the immutable peer-to-peer databases. These distributed databases remain cryptographically secured and people refer to them as Blockchains.

Bitcoin and Ethereum communities pioneered this. The improvements on the traditional Blockchain technology will consist of these:

1. **Chain code (Logic):** The traditional smart contract remains extended by the chain code. Smart contracts or self-executing agreements written in code, can interact, and trigger other smart contracts but the capabilities now become more. The important thing is that the chain code is immutable and may inherit the confidentiality or privacy. Execution of the code takes place within Docker containers that are sandboxed and may interact with hlp-fabric golang networks or with the outside world.

2. **Private transactions**: Encryptions happen on all the transaction details, volumes, assets, peers and chain code. Thereby, pattern recognition becomes impossible. This stops unauthorized leaks to people who do not belong to the network. Only when you specify a person in the network by the code, they can interact with you.

3. **Verifiable identification**: The network can set identity obfuscation but you could have a set of anonymous peers with provable identities. Each of them has a secure cryptographic technique. If the users of the network want, an auditor comes onto the scene to de-anonymize users and all their related transactions. You need this to do analysis and to conduct regulatory inspections.

4. **Customizing protocols**: You can customize any consensus protocol, as the fabric will run with any consensus mechanism such as proof-of-work, proof-of-stake and so on. This kind of customizable architectural design opens the OBC to more applications.

New use case scenarios are opening for the Blockchain. Most of these services related to the B2B platform.

Blockchain startup Digital Asset rope in IBM and Goldman Sachs

Digital Asset, which launched in 2015, has been on a mission to augment efficiency and security, settlement speed and compliance and find the way to cut spending using the Distributed Ledger Technology. Many of its products use permissioned networks that share cryptographically secure networks to put through its business logic applications. It has significance in the entire financial world. The software has the potential to cut costs, decrease risks and errors, enhance processing efficiency, offset capital need and increase security.

Since Goldman Sachs and IBM joined Digital Assets, the funding round now has $60 million from industry leaders.

Advancement in Blockchain research

Connection science is a research initiative of Massachusetts Institute of Technology. It helps build better societies through analytics and data application. It becomes the first North American academic institution to take part in a global Byzantine consensus database. In its effort to do more research into Blockchain technology, MIT is running a validator for the Ripple Consensus Ledger. This distributed ledger settles global transactions in real-time fast. This is the foundational ledger for the digital asset XRP. The work of the Ripple validator is to confirm transactions on the network.

Professor Pentland, along with David Shrier, the MD, and the MIT Connection Science will use the Internet Trust Consortium to develop financial services, enterprise data projects and other open source code projects. Further MIT Connection Science will launch Future Commerce: fintech innovation – an online course that helps entrepreneurs and executives to chart their course in financial technology disruption.

The Ripple validators are extremely lightweight and it will amount to running the server for email. The Ripple network has not reversed a single transaction in the three years of production. Thirty different world banks use the Ripple network and have closed over 30 million ledgers compared to the bitcoin that closed about 400,000 blocks.

Brian Behlendorf to become the new chief

The Hyperledger Project, launched and run by the Linux Foundation, is having a new chief in Brian Behlendorf. Brian is the Apache wizard who joins as the executive director of the Hyperledger Project. Brian, who worked with free and open source projects, knows and values the concept of open source projects. A person you can trust, the Hyperledger Project now looks to his able stewardship to 'lift all boats' as he so succinctly puts it.

Over the years, many open source visionaries have joined the Linux Foundation. Prominent among them are Chris Aniszczyk, who was with Twitter and now manages the Open Container Initiative along with the Cloud Native Computing Foundation, Sam Ramji, from the open source office of Microsoft now CEO of Cloud Foundry Foundation and Nicko van Sommeren from Good Technology and now heads the Core Infrastructure Initiative.

Behlendorf is the primary developer of the Apache Web Server. He is the founding member of the Apache Software Foundation. He has served on the Mozilla Board since 2003 and the Electronic Frontier Foundation since 2013. As per Jim Zemlin, the Linux Foundation executive director, Behlendorf will change the way the world sees the Blockchain technology.

A deeper look at Blockchain and its elements

In the context of smart contracts, the role of digital currencies remains indisputable. The role of Blockchain is that of an enabler – it helps the transactions go through. This continually updated book of records has a distributed disposition with a peer-to-peer link established at each point of the network. Tampering is impossible and strong cryptography is vital.

Elements of the Blockchain

These define the basic and useful elements of the distributed ledger network:

Digital Signatures

Here we check that the person has the private key to carry out the deal. Next, we check that the message came from the right person. We also check that no alterations occurred to the message after it left its source. The signatures allow fine-tuning to control documents and contracts.

Signed Blocks of Transactions

We keep the order of the transaction and make sure it is authentic. Here we access a higher level of fine-tuning to manipulate the transaction level. Audit trails occur in a continual way so that it becomes possible to update them all the time.

Distributed and Shared Ledger

The truth of the transaction remains established as a single version. We do not have many versions of the message. The third-party mediation remains eliminated or at least reduced. We allow the entry of autonomous agents and processes as the smart technology may include at the time.

New Strategy on Blockchain

When we think of the traditional methods of sharing information on the Internet, we think of Google docs. In this, one person prepares a document and then invites another person to share and edit it. This other person then makes the revisions and sends the document back. Until he or she does that, the first person can do nothing to view or suggest corrections during the editing process.

The banks, too, run in a similar way. They lock up the 'documents' or transactions while the interaction is underway. Until the validation takes place, one cannot see the updated record or the way the transaction went. This opened the playing field since the Internet has widened its reach and can do more.

Why should we not have a field that caters for live transactions? Why should we wait and keep one end of the deal 'locked up?' Instead of passing the documents back and forth, one could share them as we create them. Many legal contracts would benefit from this new type of dealing.

High degree of toughness

The outstanding feature of the Blockchain system is its durability and robustness. One can depend on the Blockchain and use it for conducting transactions much like the way we use the Internet for communication and sharing of documents. The inherent resilience becomes clear when one sees the way Blockchain places the document on view for the entire network. It does not belong to one person or one entity. Therefore, one single entity cannot control it.

Extending the functioning of Blockchain further, the problem of failure occurs when disruption occurs to the flow of a work function. This happens for most point-to-point transactions where we have no alternatives. However, in the Blockchain network, sharing of the document or event occurs over the network. Therefore, you cannot have any point of failure.

Many people may feel that bitcoin technology is revolutionary. In actual practice, Blockchain aims to bring everyone to "a high degree of accountability" (Ian Khan, author, Technology Futurist). In this method, one does not have any missed transactions, no human or machine errors. All transactions occur due to both the involved parties agreeing. The Blockchain establishes both the main registry where the transaction first happened and the network of connected and distributed registers with a robust validation mechanism.

Transparency guarantees corruption free network

The data embedded in the network is open. The network exists in a state of consensus, automatically checking back now and then. Reconciliation of all the transactions occurs once every ten minutes. This self-auditing ecosystem keeps updating the transactions when we add a new block. Because this block is open to the entire network, the system becomes secure. To override the entire network one needs enormous computing power. You need this to change any one bit of information without informing the system. Since such a scenario cannot take place, the data remains safe.

The opportunities for manipulation – getting more applications on the Blockchain network remains highest in nations where people do not have much wealth (Vitalik Buterin, inventor of Ethereum). We see the situation where one may download the transaction while relaying it but it exists as a second chain. This second-level chain indicates how we see the Blockchain in a new way and this opens possibilities for further development.

Now, each miner at every node is an administrator. These miners join the network of their volition and this makes the network decentralized. The incentive for participating in the network, that is the chance to win bitcoins, determines why the miners work. Here we must clarify the stand of the participating miners. They solve computational puzzles and win the bitcoins ahead of the other miners. Therefore, the term miner is not so apt but it helps to find the participants in the network. To date, we have over 700 cryptocurrencies with more in the development stages.

The concept of the distributed ledgers has already spread to the land registry and the stock market. Implementation is slow and the devices for doing so are slower in happening. The concept of decentralization has caught on for managing the entire Blockchain given to the system of computers distributed across the globe. This gives us the conviction that the decentralized networks will take the world by storm shortly (Melanie Swan, author, Blockchain: Blueprint for a New Economy).

Chapter 5:

Will Blockchain be
the Web 3.0?

The new power given to users to create value and verify digital information could result in a technology boom. So, what new applications are we looking at here?

Smart contracts

Smart contracts help avoid waste of time, as the contracts will begin executing soon as certain conditions are fulfilled. They built the open-source Blockchain project Ethereum along these lines and it shows us how it is possible. Now in its infancy, Ethereum has enormous potential to become a real game changer at a global level.

Presently, one can program the contract to do small tasks as we reach milestones. One such example is that of the financial instrument reaching a set level upon which the smart contract automatically pays a derivative to the holder of the contract. One could use the bitcoin to pay and the transaction remains completed through the Blockchain network.

Reason for using the Blockchain

You do not have to know how Blockchain works to use it. If you need to send money to some place fast, then use Blockchain. The following argument sways all others about the reasons for use. As per a World Bank estimate, money transfers sent until 2015 amounted to $430 billion.

The second big reason is that Blockchain cuts out the use of any intermediaries in the transactions. If you think back to the way the world of personal computing evolved, the first big step was the Graphical User Interface (GUI). This helped the users to get a real view of what they did in real-time. This GUI became the desktop.

Most applications designed for Blockchain take the form of a 'wallet' that people use to buy and sell. They store this wallet along with their currencies to use when they want. Since the transactions depend on who the user is, the wallet apps go along with the identity line closely. One expects the wallet apps to change in the coming few years to include different types of identities.

Increased security for data

Since the concept of decentralization is the main theme of the distributed ledgers and the Blockchain network, the risks associated with holding assets centrally does not exist. Computer hackers can only exploit the points of vulnerability as centralized points. Just as we use the password – username on the Internet, Blockchain uses encryption technology.

These exist in the form of private and public keys. This key is a randomly generated long string of numbers that becomes an address on the Internet and the user gives and gets bitcoins with the help of this address. Since the person uses the key in public, the key is a public key.

Now, there is a private key that the user can keep for making private transactions. Here, this 'password' (again this address is a randomly generated string of numbers) serves to hold the assets and bitcoins of the user. However, due to the randomness of the number generated, one cannot remember it easily. So, one should use a paper wallet. This becomes the safeguard for the user to remember his private key. If you forget this key, you will lose all the assets kept in that address.

The Internet has now an added dimension it can use to run on in addition to the traditional methods. Users can transact directly with each other instead of going through a bank. In 2016, the bitcoin transactions amounted to $200,000 per day.

Moreover, as the security increases, users are trying hard to move the banks out of the picture entirely. As stated by Goldman Sachs, Blockchain has unlimited potential to deal with the clearing and settlement. This could amount to global savings of $6 billion every year.

The Sharing Community

The sharing community has already seen success in the form of AirBnB and Uber. One can book a ride using the Uber intermediary. Payment takes place through regular online wallets but with the bitcoins and Blockchain, one can dispense with the use of banks and wallets. All that you earn goes to the online bitcoin wallet and you can make every payment through the same. This will make the sharing economy truly decentralized.

You can see the example of this in the OpenBazaar. This app connects users to others on the eBay platform. You can buy and sell just by logging into the app. You do not have to pay transaction fees when you buy and sell on eBay. Since there are no rules, the business interactions will need users to have increased personal reputation.

Crowdfunding schemes

Gofundme and Kickstarter are crowd-funding initiatives that promise big things. The peer-to-peer economy takes these initiatives to the next level. People who want to have a direct say in product and service development can now reach out directly and involve in the project.

This stood exemplified in one experiment in 2106. The Ethereum-based Decentralized Autonomous Organization (DAO) collected $200 million within two months. They did this by selling DAO tokens to the participants who got voting rights depending on how much DAO tokens they held. Though they later proved that they did this without any proper method or governance, it proved one thing. The Blockchain system could do wonderful things on a majestic scale.

Governance with distributed ledgers

One could use the distributed database technology and make transactions fully transparent. The public could get full access to all the transactions, thereby bringing in governance that was fully interactive and had the total participation of everyone. One could use the smart contracts put forward by the Ethereum chains to help automate the process.

One example of this is the Boardroom that uses Blockchain to help its users make organizational decisions. This means in real time, everything the company does and every policy and decision that it takes becomes transparent to everyone. Anyone can verify the events, transactions, and everyone will have access to information or equity.

Supply Chain Auditing

Consumers have begun to question the ethical and technical stand that product manufacturers take. Some of the stories made by the companies are true and once these undergo publication on the Blockchain, they become verifiable. One will now be more liable to buy a product whose product story he or she knows and can verify. Transparency of the type involving time stamping of products with date and place will help customers find them better. Ethical diamonds, for instance, could have a number that customers could find.

The UK-based company, Provenance, provides auditing of the supply chain for many of its products. Through the Ethereum Blockchain, they help customers make sure that their Sushi fish sold in Japan restaurants had undergone sustainable harvesting by the Indonesian suppliers.

File Storage

One of the clear advantages of decentralizing storage stands out. Distributing data over the entire Blockchain makes sure that the files will never get lost. We could upgrade the current overload on the web content delivery systems in an easy way.

The Inter Planetary File System (IPFS) brings out the point clearly. The web represents the centralized relationship between the client and the server. The IPFS gets rid of this need in the way of the bit torrent moving data around the Internet. Operation on the decentralized websites helps us move up operation speeds and decrease streaming times. This makes everything convenient.

Prediction markets

We can get a high degree of accuracy on an event by crowdsourcing predictions. Unexamined biases that make judgment inaccurate we cancel by averaging opinions. We already have many prediction markets that pay as per event outcomes. The wisdom of this technology is part of the Blockchain network. It is growing and has great potential to go to bigger heights.

Chapter 5: Will Blockchain be the Web 3.0?

One can see the Augur application, as yet in Beta, making big strides in the prediction market. It gives share offerings for predicting outcomes of real world events. If you buy into the correct prediction, you stand to gain money. If you buy more shares in the correct prediction, you get more money. One could also buy a commitment (for amounts less than a dollar) and make a market for a predicted outcome by asking a question. They collect half of the transaction fees that their market generates.

Chapter 6:

Web Identity Management

One of the prime concerns on the Internet today is the need for identity management. The ability to verify your identity online forms the basis for every successful transaction. We do have remedies for the security risk. However, these solutions are not perfect. Use of distributed ledgers helps you to secure your online identity and help you to digitize personal documents. If your online identity is secure, you can make valid online dealings. Good reputation matters and you must work to keep it up.

Developing standards for digital identity may prove to be a tough thing. Other than the technical difficulties, one must also work out a universal online identity solution that is conducive to the government and the private entities. If you think about the difference existing in the legal systems in different countries, the problem becomes doubly difficult. The little green lock or the SSL certificate denotes the e-commerce

Internet security standard. One of the new startups that aspire to create SSL standard for the Blockchain is Netki. One expects the product launch of Netki within the coming few months with a 3.5 million seed.

Protection of intellectual Property

Internet users have skill in reproducing digital information and this has increased the way Internet users use the information. They make copies of everything and distribute them without a second thought. This has led to a host of problems for the copyright holders who find their content published all over the Internet. They lose control over their intellectual property. This could lead to a serious financial loss. One could use the smart contracts to use the copyright in the copied versions of the document. The sale of copied works undergoes automation with implementing the copyright so the original owner does not suffer a loss.

To this end, we have music distribution software Mycelia that uses the Blockchain peer-to-peer distribution network. Imogen Heap, the UK singer and songwriter, founded this idea which aims to help musicians sell their music directly to their audience and send licensed samples to the producers. This will bring in royalties to music composers and songwriters and these undergo automation by the smart contract. Since the range of the Blockchain payments can exist as fractions of a bitcoin or huge amounts, the chances of success when they use Blockchain for payments remains good.

Internet of Things (IoT)

Everyone knows the Internet of Things as the virtual god of all automation. You can temperature control your garden lights, set new water levels with every coming season for your peonies, or switch on your living room lights at sunset through a clever system of interlinked electronic devices. This intricate combination of sensors, software and network helps create an exchange of data that gives the user control over his domain. Mechanisms and objects thus acquire a bigger purpose and increase system efficiency. Monitoring becomes easy leading to higher efficiency.

All the big brands in technology, telecommunication and manufacturing want to dominate the IoT sector. Samsung, AT&T, IBM and others have entered the fray with many more waiting in the wings. Because of the collaboration between the existing functionality of the gadgets and devices with the working of networking, IoT is fraught with adventure, innovation and perhaps some mischief from a few perky device manufacturers. They will control predictive maintenance, data analytics and solutions for software innovations. Imagine mass scale automation of your morning breakfast cereal!

Integrating grids in the neighborhood

You can link the neighborhood grid of renewable energy sources through the Blockchain. Ethereum based smart contracts check and change when needed so you have power when you need it. It feeds the excess power back to the grid. You can optimize your power usage through a simple program to switch off or switch on power when you reach a certain power usage limit.

ConsenSys is one of the foremost global companies that are working on several projects including those for Ethereum. One such project is the Transactive Grid that deals with distributed energy. One of the current projects involves the automation through Ethereum smart contracts of the redistribution and monitoring of microgrid energy. This is one form of the IoT smart functionality.

AML and KYC

Another system that has good potential is the anti-money laundering (AML) plan. The Know Your Customer plan (KYC) too has the same potential. Financial institutions need to go to laborious detail to get the details from each customer and record them. By incorporating the customers in the Blockchain network, the entire work becomes simple. This will cut costs and bring the needed details to the financial institutions. They could use cross-institution marking method so the customer details stand verified without undue problems. This makes the monitoring effective.

One of the new startups, Polycoin, has a KYC/AML solution. It offers to analyze transactions and in the process forwards any it feels suspicious about to the authorities and compliance officers. Another one called Tradle has introduced an application it calls Trust in Motion (TiM) that people refer to as the Instagram for KYC. People can begin to use this app straight away once they give photographs of legal documents such as a passport and utility bills to prove their identity. Once the banks verify them, the data is cryptographically stored in the Blockchain.

Data Management

Today, users of the Internet should give their personal details to use the social media websites such as the Facebook or Twitter. In the future, they can use and manage the data of their online activity. They can sell this data and make money. Since the use of bitcoin allows us to make small payments in fractions of bitcoin, this currency shows the greatest potential to find use within this system.

The personal data marketplace depends upon user privacy. Using this key concept, Enigma, a project by MIT, allows users to cryptographically encode their data and set them into small bits arranged between nodes. It allows bulk computations over the entire group so the analysis is possible. This type of fragmenting makes Enigma scalable. This is unlike Blockchain interactions where we see every step copied into the entire chain. We can expect a Beta launch of the version soon.

Land title registration

Since Blockchains make public access to documents possible for increased effectiveness in governance and use, one could access property titles under this scheme. Administering these land title registrations turns out as a labor-intensive exercise and in many instances, susceptible to fraud.

Many countries now use the Blockchain for their land registry projects. This decreases the chance of fraud happening and makes the entire thing transparent to everyone. The first government to use this was Honduras who announced their land registry scheme in 2015. We have no sign about the status of the project at present. In 2016, the Republic of Georgia struck up a contract with the Bitfury Group to develop the

Blockchain for the registration of property titles. The property rights advocate and economist, Hernando de Soto, will oversee this project. In addition, the latest to announce their intention to use Blockchain for land registry purpose is Sweden.

Stock Trading Application

The use of Blockchains for making share settlements increases the efficiency. This has led many stock exchanges to plump for the Blockchain technology. In effect, the trades become instantaneous and remove the need for intermediaries such as the custodians, auditors and clearinghouse. However, you must allow peer-to-peer communication.

The stock exchanges experimenting with Blockchain prototypes include the Japan Exchange Group (JPX), the stock exchange at Frankfurt (the Deutsche Borse) and the Australian Stock Exchange (ASX). One of the pioneering groups in this area is Linq by the NASDAQ that offers private market trading by investors in pre-IPO startups. They have struck up a partnership with Chain, a Blockchain tech company and completed their first share trade in 2015. NASDAQ recently announced another Blockchain project that uses proxy voting in the Estonian Stock Market.

Chapter 7:

Making of Block Trades

The block trade or block order refers to the sale or purchase of a huge number of securities. When one conducts a block trade, they trade a huge number of bonds or equities with another party at some pre-arranged price. This might take place out of the open market so that the force of the security price becomes less. Generally, bonds worth $200,000 or shares of stock (one does not consider penny stock) amounting to more than 10,000 will qualify as a block trade.

In the debt and equity market, the size of the block trade is huge. For this reason, individual investors rarely make this type of trade. Block trade occurs typically when a large group of institutional investors or large hedge funds buys or sells blocks through intermediaries or investment banks.

When the block trade occurs in the open market, traders exercise caution since the huge number of shares or stock will cause drastic changes in the market price of the same. For this reason, usually trading of block shares takes place through an intermediary. They do not use the services of an investment bank or a hedge fund, which is the normal procedure one uses for small amounts.

Method of block trading

We refer to the intermediary who conducts the block trades as the blockhouse. These firms specialize in large trades. They know the procedure to trade carefully so we see no volatile movement, rise or fall of the price of the commodity or security. The staff of the blockhouse have several, if not all, traders who can deal with shares and stocks of this size. These staff usually build relationships with other trading houses so they facilitate the trading of large amounts of stocks easily.

Suppose a large institution wants to conduct a block trade. They reach out to the block house staff to help them secure the best deal. After they get the order from the large institution, the staff contacts other people at the other trading houses to find the best deal. The people whom they contact are traders who specialize in making trades with that bond or stock. They will use several sellers to fill up the order they get.

Let us say HSBC wants to make a block trade of 15,000 shares at $10 per share. They contact a blockhouse. The staff at the blockhouse break the huge block into smaller chunks, which now become manageable amounts. Say, they make five smaller chunks of 3,000 shares each at $10 a share.

They assign each of these blocks to a separate broker and now the market remains stable because the amounts traded is low.

Understanding Digital Copy

Digital copy refers to the duplicate record of every confirmed bitcoin transaction ever made through a peer-to-peer network. This helps tackle the problem of double spending and incorporates safety in the bitcoin network.

Details of the digital copy

Bitcoin set the trend for cryptocurrencies in 2009. The main drive behind making the bitcoin was to have an online currency that has no central authority. The US Dollar can undergo correction of its value for inflation by the Federal Reserve. The bitcoin does not have any such authority to correct its value. No one controls the bitcoin. It operates through the decentralized ledger system, which consists of a network of independent computers distributed worldwide. These computers send the transactions to one another.

However, there was a problem known as 'double spending' in this decentralized system.

Double spending occurs when a user buys bitcoins from two sellers using the same bitcoin. To understand this concept, let us consider an example. Say, one person, Hughes, has $900 in his checking account. He links his investment to his checking account. However, he has two investment brokers Broker A and Broker B. Every time Hughes buys, the money in his checking account goes to the investment account to complete the purchase. He buys a stock worth $900 from Broker A and makes the same purchase from Broker B. Considering that the orders can undergo processing at the same time, both the Brokers will receive information that their client. Hughes, has received the stock and the funds have transferred to their accounts. However, we see Hughes received two sets of shares for his money.

Fortunately for us, we avoid the issue of double spending because the clearinghouse, banks, PayPal and other financial institutions pay and update the account balances immediately. If there have two pending transactions, they put one of them on hold so that the issue of the account balance being the same for both the transactions does not occur. Bitcoin solves this problem on the distributed ledger system by issuing the copies of the transactions to multiple miners on the network. Since all the miners must confirm the transactions on the network the problem of duplication does not arise.

Blockchain is the ledger that records each of these transactions of the bitcoin. The copies of this undergo distribution to all the users on the decentralized network. Manipulative users might try to spend the bitcoin twice and they avoid this by issuing copies of the entire holding to everyone to the entire network system. Bitcoin users verify each transaction and add them to the distributed ledgers.

Suppose one miner is the first to verify a transaction. He adds it to his queue of new transactions that they must add to the new ledger. Then, he publishes his result. The next miner will verify the result published by the first miner and then add the transaction to the ledger queue in their digital copy. Transactions become final and permanently recorded on Blockchain after six miners confirm the transaction. This shows that the user has funds needed to carry out the deal.

When we see the example shown above, the first miner may record the transaction Hughes makes with Broker A as legitimate and then publish his result. However, when the miner sees the second transaction Hughes makes with Broker B, he notices the lack of funds and marks the transaction as not legitimate. When other miners copy the transaction, they will all mark the first transaction with Broker A as final and recorded in the ledger. You could say the miners are clearing houses for bitcoin transactions.

Since we have the digital copies of the transactions, we have very little chance that the transaction history of the entire ledger stands compromised. Any user wishing to manipulate the ledger transaction will only have his or her own copy of the ledger to manipulate. If they need to change the transaction history of the entire distributed ledger, they need to have access to everyone's copy of the ledger, which seems an improbable occurrence.

Chapter 8:

A Look at Bitcoin Block

In this context, let us look at the bitcoin - the digital currency created in 2009 by the mysterious Satoshi Nakamoto. Until now, the identity of this Satoshi Nakamoto remains unknown. However, bitcoin transactions promise lower fees and complete decentralized authority unlike other online payment processors and banks.

You do not have any physical bitcoins. You only have bitcoin balances kept on online addresses using private and public keys. A huge network of computers amounting to massive computing power verifies these transactions at all time. To refresh, these keys are Internet addresses, which are very long strings of numbers generated through a mathematical encryption algorithm and compares to the bank account number you use for your financial transactions. Each user also has a private key that they use to authorize bitcoin transactions. You could compare this to the ATM pin.

Chapter 8: A Look at Bitcoin Block

The IRS issued a statement in March 2014 stating they would tax bitcoin as property and not as currency. Thus, gains and losses on the bitcoin holding become capital gains and losses but if you hold the bitcoin in inventory, they will have ordinary gains and losses.

Groups of individuals or companies hold the governing power in the network of computers. They become the miners. The driving force for these miners is the transaction fees and mining rewards. Mining rewards are usually the release of new bitcoins. The network pays the transaction fees. We could think of the miners as the decentralized authority that authenticates the entire network. The release of new bitcoins takes place at a periodically declining rate in a way the total supply of bitcoins moves toward 21 million.

You can divide the bitcoin to eight decimal places meaning the smallest (the Satoshi) has the value of one in one hundred million of one bitcoin. If the participating miners need and accept more divisions of the bitcoin, then you can divide the bitcoin to even more decimal places. Here we note that the bitcoin in lowercase refers to the currency while the Bitcoin in upper case denotes the concept. We can refer to the plural as bitcoin or bitcoins. The abbreviated form is BTC or rarely XBT.

Tracking the bitcoin block

A lot of activity occurs on the Bitcoin network. This consists of the records of the transactions initiated by each miner. The records go into a file on the network called a block. Let us compare this activity to the bank transactions. All the records of the bank are like a Blockchain. One transaction, say you make a cash withdrawal, would be one block. This means that the block bears the relationship of one part to the whole in the Blockchain.

The block represents the present and holds the way forward to the future. If a new transaction takes place, the present block gives way to the new block that records the transaction. When they complete the block, it becomes the permanent record of the transactions. The system operates in a cyclic manner pushing new blocks and transferring the data from the old ones to the new ones. Thus, each of the blocks can have several the transactions made until now.

Each of the blocks has a mathematical problem linked to it. Miners compete to find out the problem and solve it. The miner who completely solves the puzzle wins the Bitcoin race. They get bitcoin rewards as the incentive to compete further. The winning miner shares his or her answer with the rest of the participating miners. Once they confirm it, they record the answer on the block.

Every winning miner gets 25 BTC as the reward. This then enters the bitcoin circulation. This reward becomes the first entry in the new block created on the Bitcoin network. One cannot give new blocks to the network without the answer. Therefore, the answer regulates how you make the new bitcoins and the difficulty of the answer determines the number of bitcoins generated. On an average, it takes about 10 minutes for the miners in the network to find the solution; therefore, it takes 10 minutes to create 25 BTC.

Hypothetical attack on the Blockchain

For any attack on the Blockchain to occur, the miners who exist in the system must have majority control. This means they must represent at least 51% of those present in the network. Say, a miners group constituting 50% or more blocks the confirmations of new transactions because they control the networks mining hash rate. They halt payment on some (or all) of the users. They can reverse the transactions on some or all the blocks. This gives them the power to double-spend the bitcoins. However, since they cannot create new bitcoins or change the old blocks (records), they will not destroy the bitcoins. Nevertheless, we will feel the damage.

Dealing with the attack

Cryptocurrencies such as the bitcoin rely on the distributed ledger systems such as the Blockchains. These ledgers record every deal made on the network and make them available for all users there. Since this occurs instantaneously, you cannot spend the same bitcoin or cryptocurrency twice. Such a happening will destroy the faith and make the use of cryptocurrency obsolete.

Each of the blocks has links to the earlier and a new block summarily means that the old one has undergone validation. They recorded the old one and the new transaction has resulted in the making of a new block. The network user will quickly spot any fraudulent transactions and reject them.

However, once a group gets 51% control over the network, they can block the process of validating of new blocks. Other miners who complete blocks will not get the required authentication. They will only allow their group members to create new blocks thus getting a monopoly on the creation of fresh blocks. They will thus walk away with the rewards, which at the second stage are 12.5 and will progressively drop down to zero.

Among the many ways they can cheat the system, the first one is to block the others. The second one is to make a transaction and go on to reverse it. It now appears as if they still have the bitcoins they sent on the transaction. This is the double-spending vulnerability that the distributed ledger must prevent.

If one suspects that an attack is about to happen, then we could lock the transactions. Then, even if the attackers had 51% control, they would find it difficult to alter the historical blocks. Moreover, if we make the locks very much back in time, they become that much harder to break. You see at each of the checkpoints, the system hard-codes the transactions into the software of the currency.

On a note of interest, the website ghash.io went over the 50% mark of the computing power of the bitcoin in July 2104. They then reduced their stake in the pool and promised not to exceed 40% of the total share. In another unrelated incident, both Shift and Krypton underwent 51% attacks. These networks have their basis on the Ethereum network.

Chapter 9:

Coin Mixing and Coinjoin

To increase the privacy of the bitcoin users, a novel anonymization strategy came into force called the Coinjoin. Multiple users on the network sign an agreement to mix their coins and use it for separate bitcoin transactions. This process known as coin mixing helps address privacy concerns adequately.

Coinjoin represents an advancement in technology in the field of digital tools that helps companies interact at a higher level with their customers. All the online retail platforms, mobile devices and social media increased the data supply accompanying the shift of the traditional forms to digital forms. The influx of technology in various fields of storing, sharing, as well as gathering, data helped companies gather large amounts of data and store them without incurring much cost. However, the extensive accessibility of data makes them less secure. People worry about the data privacy and the way they do online transactions remains affected due to this. Individuals seek an anonymous way to interact online because the online transactions leave a digital trail. At first, users assumed Bitcoin would solve the problems of privacy adequately.

Bitcoin transactions remain secure but not anonymous. Since the bitcoin ledger remains publicly accessible, one can trace the transactions others have made. They only need to tap into one of the nodes in the network and access a copy of the records. This transparent nature of the Bitcoin ledgers allows anyone to use information in the public domain, uses the IP address to find out the identity of the user. One thus gets to know what they transacted in, during their last outing.

This led to the birth of Coinjoin, an identity obfuscation technique designed to hide the identity of the Blockchain users. The first step to using the Coinjoin is to find another user who wants to mix coins with you. Both start a joint transaction together. The term input refers to the address from where you send bitcoins and output refers to the address to where the bitcoins will reach.

Hackers can find each input and output. However, when one uses the Coinjoin, several inputs and outputs combine as one input and one output. Hackers can no longer find the single inputs and outputs. For instance, check this example. A user A buys the commodity from user B. C buys from D while E purchases an item from F. Without Coinjoin, these transactions become three separate deals and anyone can see the input and output. With Coinjoin, all the purchases become one purchase and all the outputs become one output. Now, there is only one transaction without any clear sign of who got what from whom. You have several digital tools that use anonymization processes such as SharedCoins, JoinMarket, and Dark Wallet.

The Process of Bitcoin Mining

The main activity in the bitcoin mining process is the identification and verification of transactions followed by their addition to the public ledger. This adds a new block to the Blockchain and the process releases new bitcoins. Here you compile all recent transactions into blocks and in the process, the miners solve a difficult computational challenge. The first person to solve the puzzle gets to place the first block in the next chain. He thus gets the rewards for the solution. These rewards serve to give the incentives for the mining process and keep the Blockchain growing. It involves both transaction fees as well as the newly released bitcoins.

Details of the mining process

Block reward is the number of new bitcoins released after they have mined the block. They make the block reward half once in every 4 years or so which amounts to 210,000 blocks. The block rewards that began as 50 BTC in 2009, became 25 in 2014, will continue to decrease. It will result in a total release of bitcoin rewards amounting to 21 million.

How does the hardness of the puzzles of the mining network affect the result? The network has its input and the continuing effort will help solve the hard puzzles. One can adjust the difficulty of the blocks and they do so once in every 2016 block or roughly every 2 weeks. The principle underlying this type of adjustment of the difficulty is to keep the rate of the discovery of the block a constant. Therefore, when some more computational power comes into play in the mining, the difficulty will adjust to a higher level making mining more difficult. Similarly, when the computational power decreases, the mining difficulty decreases.

In the days when mining just began, normal desktop CPUs did all the computational work. As time passed, it became obvious that use of graphic cards and graphic user interfaces (GPUs) made the process simpler. After a while, they made the Application Specific Integrated Circuit (ASIC) with the specific purpose of doing the mining.

The first one came into operation in 2013 and the subsequent ones kept increasing in efficiency. Since mining is a competitive field, only those with the latest ASICs stand to win bitcoins. If one uses CPUs, GPUs, or older model ASICs, the cost of mining becomes more than the income one gets.

Proof of work

In this system, a tangible effort goes into deterring any malicious or frivolous use of computing power. These frivolous acts might consist of sending spam e-mail or initiating the denial of service attacks. In 2004, Hal Finney adapted this for use with money in the reusable proof of work idea. Once bitcoin entered the scene, it adopted the idea and Finney received the money made from the first bitcoin transaction. Most of the other cryptocurrencies use the proof of work in one form or the other.

In practice, users can detect tampering with a long string of numbers known as hashes and these become the proof of work. Bitcoin uses the hash function SHA-256. When we put a series of data through the hash function, it will generate only one hash. However, when we change any one part of the original data, the avalanche effect will result in the creation of a new hash that is very different from the original.

Regardless of the size of the original dataset, the hash generated by the given function will result in one having the same length. However, the hash function only works one way. You cannot use a hash to get the original data set. You may only check that it matches with the original data set.

You can set any hash for a set of bitcoin transactions using a modern computer. That is why we have the level of difficulty. The process now becomes work and they adjust the setting as the miners mine the block. They reset the difficulty once in every ten minutes on an average.

First, they set a target for the hash. If the target is low and the set of valid hashes is small, it becomes difficult to generate one. What it means is this type of hash begins with a long set of zeroes. The block has a fixed number of transactions and amount of transactions. If we changed the transaction amount by even 0.00001BTC, the hash will become unrecognizable and the network will reject the hash as a fraud.

Every set of data can only generate one hash. To make sure that the hash they generate is below the target, the miners use a 'nonce' integer. This nonce is the number used once only. Upon reaching a valid hash, they broadcast it to the network. Then, they add the block to the network.

Though mining is competitive, the chances of winning are more due to chance. Anybody can win and often the miners will pool together to increase their chances of winning. This helps them mine more blocks, get more transaction fees, and for newly generated blocks, the new bitcoins.

Proof of work makes it difficult to alter any of the transactions on the network since alterations would involve re-mining the entire block. Thus, one miner cannot monopolize the computing power of the network. This is due to the high cost of the machinery and the power needed to complete the hash functions.

Entry of the RMBCoin in China

China does not seem to have had much involvement with the Bitcoin. However, they have worked on the national digital currency project the RMBCoin. Users of the RMBCoin will not have access to private keys and one is not sure where the PBOC is going with its national digital currency.

The aim of the PBOC seems to point to the aim of letting people control their currency in a digital and easy way. That would make them work in the same way that the banks work today. However, RMBCoin will use the Blockchain technology to control and issue the coin.

The PBOC investigated many bitcoin exchanges and made many positive changes. The view of the experts is that one does not expect too many things when they have a national digital currency in opposition to the bitcoin currency. In fact, many countries have their own digital currencies. The United Kingdom had made a beginning in the direction of a national digital currency but it seems to have stalled on the way. Undoubtedly, other countries too will explore the possibility of having their own national digital currency as well.

Though many Bitcoin enthusiasts may feel let down, the effect of RMBCoin on the trading market should not make too many waves. The PBOC removed the leveraged margin trading for the bitcoin. Now, it wants to introduce its currency in the mainstream. While people in the cryptocurrency world may not express surprise, they remain curious, to say the least. Imitation is the best form of flattery but will there be more? One must wait and see.

Ricochet makes snooping into bitcoin harder

Bitcoin users always like it when software companies make things in the wallets and banks that favor their adaptability. In this respect, the Ricochet feature of the Samourai Wallet improves the bitcoin sustainability.

The Samourai Wallet is famous for its efforts at making the wallet more private and anonymous. They mock anyone who spies on the bitcoin. Blockchain knocks them out of the ballpark. This new feature will help users avoid any form of unnecessary government scrutiny.

The Samourai Wallet announced that they flag thousands of bitcoin transactions as suspicious every day. They did not show the source of this information but these flagged transactions could pose problems for bitcoin users. Big companies that use bitcoin transactions too will find many difficulties.

Bitcoin exchanges regularly suspend accounts and freeze funds if they feel some account is not above suspicion in their view. They reserve the right to term any account as suspicious. Coinbase did this sort of thing and got a lot of negative feedback from the users. Coinbase is working at restoring the individual accounts of users.

To determine suspicious activity, investigators look at the origin of funds going back five levels. Therefore, it does not matter where or how you spend the money, it falls under 'suspicious' if the origin remains tainted.

The Samourai Wallet developed this new tool, Ricochet, which adds four new levels to each transaction. This forces the Blockchain spies to work more adding to the operating costs.

Chapter 9: Coin Mixing and Coinjoin

However, the fact remains that the bitcoin wallet will have added privacy. In its testing phase now, the Samourai Wallet promises to have many more features soon.

Chapter 10:

The MIT Technology Review invites you to The Business of Blockchain

This one-day conference takes place on April 18, 2017, to explore the challenges and opportunities that Blockchain faces. The event will occur at the MIT Media Lab.

MIT Media Lab Digital Currency Initiative is the leading research center in this field. They will open the topics related to Blockchains and public digital ledgers. Most people know about Blockchain only when they used the bitcoin. Obviously, bitcoin records transactions to resist counterfeiting.

This technology proves useful for people who do not know each other and need an intermediary to conduct transactions in the ordinary course of events. Most of the people use banks.

However, of late, governments, companies and researchers consider how to shut out the intermediary and indulge in a range of commercial activities including energy, supply chains, public services, banking and much more.

When these ideas materialize, customers will not consider this as another option but as one of the main instruments for operation in the financial world. This could involve tracking goods or exchange of money, transfer of sensitive information, technologies to create and open new frontiers in markets and unprecedented speeds of operation along with the reputed transparency.

Top Blockchain Possible Applications

Increasing possibilities with the Blockchain

The importance of Bitcoin in our life is not yet tangible but it has undoubtedly changed the flow of progress either in a positive or negative way. First, we must accept that we can find a use for it in every sphere of our lives.

This realization makes it as big - if not bigger - than the Internet of Things (IoT). In addition, it might evolve into the Internet ledger of everything. Many people feel that we give excessive attention without getting any materialization. The question 'when' seems more significant than 'what' at this present juncture.

Use of Blockchain for governing countries

The use of distributed ledgers in the governance of countries may seem a colossal task at this stage. However, the way we see the system heading the dominance of the decentralized power gaining prominence over the rest of the guiding forces seems inevitable. This makes Blockchain one of the top contenders for the place of authority.

However, demarking the limits of the power and assigning some real values of geographical locations or landmarks seems to present the challenge. The government always seems to lag behind with respect to collaboration with advancements in scientific progress. Proper alignment of the financial sector with the scientific community should solve the problem. What this points to is the need for a smart ledger that dictates the policies of the government as a pre-selected aim for all matters related to the running of the state.

Use in legal fields

You could extend the Blockchain in a way so that anyone could have access to the laws of the land. If you combine it with methods of providing online proof of law breaking, the chances that anyone would ever break the law again is bleak. This would need extensive frameworks covering every aspect of the law and it should have applicability to the sub-territories where one wants to apply the law. The use of smart contracts brings a new dimension to the realm. Online firms could offer their ability in various fields of real estate, finance, business and commercial activity such that one could buy a smart contract from them for a price. Once they enforced that smart contract, the property or business of the person came under the legal protection of the smart contract. It all depends on what you are selling and whether you need such a smart contract.

You could create a verifiable audit to use for your insurance claims. It helps you keep track of the purchases, either in a date wise ledger or in a ledger related to some online store like Amazon. It helps when the company you work for refunds purchases made towards some project.

In this respect, one sees the work of Tierion as showing good promise for new entrepreneurs who want to explore the field of online Blockchain storage. Beginners could get a feel of the Blockchain and realize its full potential by trying out their free plan first. This could help you with your claims on the health bills.

Applications to the field of health

One could track the onset and spread of infections on a worldwide scale using Blockchains. This will help one understand the nature of the infections better and place markers so one can prepare for the next infection attack. One could make links to worldwide relief agencies and make provisions for the sharing of information about the infection. One could target payments and donations with good accuracy with the Blockchain.

The use of a separate online coin for the health sector shows good chances of proving useful. They have proposed to make a coin named Genomecoin for the use with the Genomic Data Commons (GDC). The GDC in partnership with the NCI would give access to a huge database, which one could use through the Blockchain. The use of a coin for one database seems to drive the purpose of decentralized authority far away. However, we see possibilities.

In another example, we see how effective DNA bits prove for providing solutions. This organization based in Israel helps give help for clinical data and genetic samples. They track and cross-reference the facts to help treat patients and anonymously authenticate health-related data.

Fees for trading bitcoins in Chinese exchanges

You must pay 0.2% trading fees from now on in Chinese bitcoin exchanges for each transaction. Just a few days back, the OKCoin, BTCC and Huobi stopped leveraged trades for Chinese users. From now on, the three exchanges will charge the transaction fee. The announcement said that this payment would come into force from midday of Tuesday January 24, 2017, onwards.

The statement read that they charge the fee to curb the extreme volatility and manipulation of the market. Huobi stated this on its website too. OKCoin made the same announcement on its website. The central bank is scrutinizing the activities of the three bitcoin exchanges now. It seems they had planned and made the statement ready together as they released the announcement at the same time.

Margins and futures trading came to a halt last week and the BTCC CEO Bobby Lee said that traders might have to pay fees. He said that the three exchanges had planned it. Following this, a fourth exchange. Yunbi, based in Beijing, said that it too would charge trading fees to prevent speculation. It aims at preventing sharp price fluctuation of the bitcoin. They would only levy a fee on the trades and all other bitcoin services will remain unaffected by the fee.

One news agency reported that the PBOC did not explicitly demand the trader fee. However, the PBOC did want to see less volatility in the market for bitcoin trading. This action by the exchanges helped to curb the volatility. These changes did not affect the value of the cryptocurrency.

The present price of the bitcoin to dollar remained steady at $921.22 on the Bitstamp Price Index (BPI). Following the announcement, the price of the bitcoin fell to a low of $892.27 after which it went up to $397.74. However, towards the end of the day, it settled to its present mark.

One can expect changes in the trading volumes tomorrow due to the announcement. However, we must see what change it will make to the bitcoin. Chinese traders do not have an alternate cryptocurrency. Nor do they have any Blockchain type of assets. People do hope that the no-transaction-fee trade will appear again though there is no telling if this will ever happen. Meantime, the other international exchanges may find this an opportune moment to revise their own trading fees.

Chapter 11:

US Should Move to Digital Currency

The World Economic Forum held its annual meeting at Davos in Switzerland. They had a meeting called Ending Corruption where the Economics Nobel Prize winner, Joseph Stiglitz, expressed his opinion that phasing out fiat currency and moving towards digital currency has more advantages than disadvantages.

He spoke about the lack of transparency in the global finance markets and of the existence of the global framework for corruption and tax avoidance. He added that people were more likely to seek out these secret havens and indulge in activity there. If these havens did not exist, then the benefits would vanish and to this extent, he wanted the US to move towards digital currency.

Chapter 11: US Should Move to Digital Currency

Though there remained the issues of cyber security and privacy, adopting a digital currency would prove useful for a country like the USA. They must make the move overcoming transitional issues he said. Stiglitz remains a staunch anti-corruption campaigner in that in September last year, he attended a public event at the London School of Economics where he stated that US government did the right thing in shutting down the use of bitcoin as people used it to avoid regulation and tax payment. Of course, now he wants the opposite thing, namely open the bitcoin, but his aim remains the same, uprooting corruption.

People see his stand against the International Monetary Fund (IMF) for past economic crises as his opposition to the banking setup. He seems eager to see the fiat currency shown the door. He joins an elite group of people of whom Harvard professor Kenneth Rogoff is one. Rogoff states that the economic ailment in society would greatly diminish if one reduced the amount of physical currency in society.

In India, the Prime Minister, Narendra Modi, has removed 90% of the currency from circulation and this has paved the way forward towards a cashless society. He did this by removing the Rs 500 and Rs 1,000 notes as this helps to curb terrorism, corruption, and tax evasion.

Preparing for the Internet of Things explosion

The amount of data is witnessing an exponential increase. Things will come to the fore by 2020 when you will have 50 billion devices online. All these devices will send, pass on, receive and decode data and if one considers costs, these will take astronomical values. The Blockchain, with its widening reach and low costs, will prove the ideal solution to solving the data problem. The data would stay accessible, secure, and reliable, as tampering is not possible.

The issue of tracking and managing billions of devices remains. However, technology grows and so it will surely come up with an answer. This must happen before the commercial aspects of the Internet of Things get a grip on our Internet interactions. The Blockchain system will give an easy way for the makers of IoT devices to deal with tracking, deploying and harnessing the true power of the IoT devices. The decentralized system would open the scope of operation enormously.

In this respect, one could see people deploy connected vehicles, use of smart appliances, and deployment of smart sensors in the supply chain among many other things. Obviously, the connected vehicles could easily avoid accidents, follow an online traffic regulation program to ease traffic congestion, find the best speed to help optimize petrol consumption, and so on.

Smart sensors in the supply chain could help users find when a product becomes available in the mall, or when the price of a commodity drops, and so on. One could use the smart contracts to buy the product when such an occurrence happens. Alternately, one could trigger the sale of your own brand when this event happens.

We will never see the end of the use of smart devices in the household and at the workplace. We have not seen many things in action on a regular basis other than automatic garage doors, and garden lights. The drawback here may be in trying to use the Smartphone to control these devices and not let the Blockchain do its thing.

Most Influential TV Show in China features Bitcoin

Bitcoin popularity in China continues to rise. The talk show featuring the latest cutting-edge financial news included talk about the bitcoin. The topic was whether bitcoin was a Ponzi scheme or not.

One of China's leading economists, Larry Hsien Ping Lang, talked about the topic and said that bitcoin was worthless. When Baidu, the Google of China, announced that they would accept bitcoin payments, the price of the cryptocurrency shot up. The CEO of BTC China, Bobby Lee offered 100 BTC to Larry Lang, who refused to take it. This is worth some $90,000 at the current market price.

Another economist said that bitcoin is the currency of the future. In Chinese exchanges, the price of bitcoin more than quadrupled. This raised the price of the bitcoin and it reached values compared to the western exchanges. However, the price crashed within minutes locking out many traders for lack of funds. The PBOC decided to investigate the freeze of the exchanges during the fast movement of the price. However, this seems more of words than action as PBOC does not favor the bitcoin.

In 2013, the bitcoin price surpassed the gold parity in the Chinese exchanges. The PBOC banned the bitcoin payments forcing Baidu to abandon its service. Recently, they prevented exchanges from offering margins and forced private trading companies to pay the trading fees. It seems to many that the PBOC wants bitcoin to have a lower price.

Lee, on his part, asked traders to trade in mBTC to show the lower price of the bitcoin. This would appease regulators, he said. This follows rumors that the Chinese exchange OKCoin.cn does not allow non-Chinese traders. This protectionist action must have originated from the PBOC.

Many people think that this action by the PBOC reflects the harsh circumstances that the people of China face. Further, in trying to suppress the bitcoin, the Chinese authorities interfere with a globally free cryptocurrency that could be the currency of the future.

Lower profit for banks due to digitization

The profits of the European banks are under threat. Half of it may be lost by 2020 due to digitization. Most of the developed markets in the United Kingdom and Europe have a risk attached to one-third or so of their profits, which now amounts to $35 billion. Digital disruption is the culprit and the profits of the banks that stand at $110 billion could become a mere $50 billion.

The US banks seem to have a good method to tackle these digital disruptions. The Japanese banks have $1 billion and US banks have $45 billion at risk. Yet, the profitability would drop only to 8% for the US banks and 5% for the Japanese banks. The pressure of digitization would cut the profit margins but boosts competition.

In the emerging markets, China and India seem to have lost ground to the digital commerce concerns. They are taking over the banking sector. The threat to the banking sector is real with tech firms inserting themselves between the customers and the banks and capturing the essential customer relationships for their own concerns.

Chapter 12:

Comparing Blockchain and Bitcoin

Do the two entities match each other?

Blockchain and Bitcoin have emerged as world-changing concepts that show the path forward. Therefore, when we compare the two we see many similarities and a few differences. We see the most obvious thing about the cryptocurrency as a virtual currency. It does not have a physical form and so one may only see its representation online. Everyone accepts it as a valid token for an exchange of value.

In so much that a few governments have started its use to register land deals, the lure must surely be in its decentralized nature – everyone can share it, even those who are not involved in the land deal. They act as record keepers. The thrill of being there and doing it now has permeated to others who dare to take up the challenge of doing the 'mining' work.

The miners in the Blockchain again exist more in concept than as people with pickaxes and shovels shoveling dirt. Yet, the Blockchain would not exist without the miners. In this respect, both Blockchain and the bitcoin have a mystical aura about them – they both seem like the Peter Pan who disappears into the ether after he does the work.

There is no printing of the currency, only a record of the transaction. This establishes the virtual existence of the currency. The miners who get the share of the Bitcoins start a new trail forward. The rest of the miners follow behind, to win another day. They maintain control over the cryptocurrency by keeping the total coins in circulation to 21 million.

This kind of change - that changes the other - keeps both the entities moving. In addition, even as we discuss this, the value of the bitcoin is showing signs of touching the old $1000 mark it broke back in 2013.

Rise of the cryptocurrencies

We see the complete domination of the cryptocurrency sector by bitcoin and Ether. More interest in the bitcoin technology has arisen due to the attention big tech firms such as Microsoft, Amazon, and IBM gives it. Let us go back a few years to when the cryptocurrency was not as famous as it is today.

Lazlo bought two pizzas for 10,000 bitcoins in May 2010. At that time, bitcoins were not worth anything much. Today, those 10,000 bitcoins would have a value of over $9 million. Today, many banks, such as Citigroup and JP Morgan Chase, have begun to invest in Blockchain technology.

Though cryptocurrencies raise doubts in the minds of people, bitcoin seems to have surpassed the initial misgivings. Trading at close to $1000 now, the bitcoin now is more impressive than ever. One can hardly ignore a financial instrument that has such a high value.

The reason for this is twofold. One is the global shortage of fiat cash such as in Venezuela where the inflation has put the people into a quandary. They need bundles of money to buy food. At the other end of the spectrum, countries such as India have moved rapidly toward demonetizing fiat currencies and have shifted towards online wallets for payments. People now see the digital currency as the only real savior and they want more of it.

People work on many common online projects such as the Hyperledger Project, Gem Health Network and Corda by R3 CEV. Though one does not see the rush of results, we need to push the global monetization through the Blockchain network, and we have hope that things will soon stand resolved.

Impact of SegWit on bitcoin

Undoubtedly, the core developers of the bitcoin have gone through much pain but they have finally added SegWit to the bitcoin network. SegWit is Segregated Witness that helps faster block validation. For the same block size, you see a higher turnover of transactions. The SegWit upgrade uses the Lightning Network to go ahead with off-chain transactions. This helps wallet software developers. Using the Lightning Network, you can make Blockchains fast and scale them easily. The willingness to adopt SegWit is downbeat in some mining groups. They want an increase in the block size and want trade-offs. However, we do not see any sustained resistance to SegWit.

Though we do not see much increase in the number of people who use bitcoins regularly, the price of bitcoin continues to increase. The change spending seems to show the use of bitcoins for capital migrancy. For instance, since the people fear that the RMB may lose value, they convert their holdings into cryptocurrencies, which show a steady value on the market.

This brings the currency exchanges into focus since the traditional banking feels the impact of cryptocurrencies. These exchanges allow for the easy passage of various currencies. Further, the risk remains localized in the exchanges and though many hacks and thieves will try to do their best, the risk will not spread. The reason for this is that the amount of money that passes through the exchange is predictable.

You might have instances when the regulators view consumer protection and identity confirmation as priorities. They might even in extreme cases, disallow transactions as it happened with Colbitex. The Columbian government closed the cryptocurrency in August saying that it had no real substance. Nevertheless, the reality of the emergence of cryptocurrencies remains to that extent where governments begin to use them as legal tender for their various schemes.

Blockchain development team of Deloitte show Proof of Concept

The Block of Ireland undertook a trial to set up the Proof of Concept with the development team of Blockchain. They aimed to show that we could carry out the Blockchain technology. They did this by adding the data as an accessible layer to existing systems. The test proved successful.

Deloitte has increased the investment in the development and research of Blockchain applications. Their clients become the beneficiaries of all this effort. So far, they say, they have developed over 30 prototypes of Blockchain applications in various fields such as rewards solutions, cross-border payments and digital banking.

The firm, Deloitte, claims to have over 800 professionals working across 20 countries. One of the global Blockchain teams, known as Deloitte's Rubix helped install a bitcoin ATM in Canada. They are opening a new Blockchain lab as part of the Blockchain development "Grid" of Deloitte. At the start of this year, they opened their Blockchain lab at New York. They will open more labs during the year.

The Deloitte Financial Services partner, David Dalton, heads the Dublin Blockchain lab. The impact of these labs will go beyond the financial realm he anticipated. By adopting the Blockchain technology, he says, organizations could bring radical change to the way they work and interact with their customers.

This new lab in Dublin in the EMEA region (Europe, Middle East and Africa) is in the Silicon Docks district, the region where you have industry giants such as Facebook and Google. At present, they have a team of 25 designers and developers but expect to increase the size to 50 shortly.

Trading and banking with the Blockchain

The time is surely shifting for those who stick to their guns and Coinbase will know it. They have staunchly supported the use of bitcoin. Treading on the Blockchain remains a challenge mainly because of the unscrupulous traders who keep coming up with schemes to swindle people. Due to its transparency, Blockchain offers many opportunities for cheating. The anonymous and unregulated nature contributes to the openness but ushers in a share of corrupt people.

The figures on Blockchain and the bitcoin show how big they have grown. Now, we have $20 billion worth of bitcoins. People predict that within the coming ten years, we will see a shift in the way countries store their currencies. They expect a large shift as much as 10% of the GDP.

In this context, the capital market spending on bitcoins increased from $30 million in 2014 to $75 million and $129 million in the following two years. From there, it rose to $210 million in 2017 (as an estimate). The estimated values for the coming two years are $313 million and $400 million.

JP Morgan, Goldman Sachs, and Bank of America have taken a great interest in the Blockchain technology. Blockchain has a 'cleaner' record than bitcoin and so the financial institutions prefer to work with Blockchain. They formed a coalition to help induct the Blockchain practices into the mainstream of banking practices. Many other financial institutions such as the Citi, NASDAQ, and Visa have become ready to take part in the Blockchain operations.

The reason for the huge attraction that Blockchain has for banks is clear. The banks want to increase the efficiency of their financial transactions. They use their permissioned Blockchains to keep up records of dealings with clients. They do this with software that they need to update once in every three or four years.

Experts feel that banks must not merely try to increase their banking capabilities but bring a change in the way people view the banking practice. One knows already how easy it is to transact huge amounts of money quickly using the Blockchain.

An overview of new Bitcoin startups

The Circle is a service that allows the use of its transfer services to efficiently transfer money using bitcoins alone to anyone, anywhere. You can hold, deposit or send money. Bitreserve is another startup that uses bitcoin during its starting phase. Users can now convert currencies and change to four types of metals too.

These companies, in due course, will adopt Blockchain and broaden their financial services. Bitreserve has changed its name to Uphold. Users can make deposits in any currency now. Circle now allows the use of debit and credit cards. Many startups allowed the use of other currency since they too did not want to become too much bitcoin dependent. The other reason was that bitcoin became a bad currency for a while.

However, the use of all currencies opens the businesses and gives everyone some leeway in their commercial dealings. Blockchain is clean and so holds the interest of all businesses and banks alike. For players in the commercial sector, concentrating on the positive aspects of the Blockchain could mark the upturn of their businesses. It offers the opportunity for making headways in new directions and putting their businesses on top of the competition.

Cybersecurity and Blockchain

On the Internet, hackers can use the single points of failure to steal and spoof identities, use cyber traps to rob vital personal information and shut down entire networks. They can then tamper with the data and carry out other cunning attacks.

Chapter 12: Comparing Blockchain and Bitcoin

Since Blockchain uses an alternative approach to storing and using data, it provides a good way out of the cyber spoof-up mess. One could now prevent security incidents and cyber-attacks using Bitcoin and Ethereum.

The first area would be in the protecting data integrity. The process consists of using private keys so the source of the data is always verifiable. Second, we use detailed methods to prove that nobody had tampered with the keys. Here the accent is not on secrecy but on making the news public. The entire network knows the news and shares the news. Thus, any one person cannot change the key or the data.

The second area is in protecting the identities. Public Key Infrastructure (PKI) is a method of using cryptography for public keys, messaging apps, emails, and more. The PKI relies on third-party Certified Authorities. Therefore, there is every chance that hackers can crack encryptions and steal data and identities.

However, Blockchain eliminates the risk of false key use and verifies identity securely. CertCoin is one of the first to use Blockchain PKI. This application developed by MIT removes the use of central authority altogether. Therefore, there does not exist any single point of failure.

Conclusion

Bitcoin has made it to the other shore. You now have more information throughout this book, *"Blockchain: The Untapped Goldmine of Blockchain that Virtually No One Knows About."* Though we had some worries about the security, it sailed through on the robustness of Blockchain and its own integral value.

Having become a path for the future, Blockchain needs many more corrections and adaptations. Undoubtedly, most of these will come from the users who see the need for change. Nevertheless, we must ride the wind and the waves and not fight it.

We have included much about the approach of businesses toward Blockchain in this book. They show how the new world will take the old world and dump it by the wayside. The new order is now yours and mine. Dare we move forward and gain from this new form of sharing? I think we should!

References

IBM Blockchain http://www.ibm.com/blockchain/

Hyperledger https://www.hyperledger.org/

The Linux Foundation
https://www.linuxfoundation.org/news-
media/announcements/2016/02/linux-foundation-s-
hyperledger-project-announces-30-founding

Wikipedia https://en.wikipedia.org/wiki/Hyperledger

Bitcoin https://bitcoin.org/en/

Blockchain Technologies
http://www.blockchaintechnologies.com/blockchain-
applications

Cryptocoins news
https://www.cryptocoinsnews.com/blockchain-news/

Blockchain News http://www.the-blockchain.com/

Bernard Marr Forbes / Tech / #Big Data
http://www.forbes.com/sites/bernardmarr/2017/01/24/a-
complete-beginners-guide-to-blockchain/#c1cae8366a6f

www.ingramcontent.com/pod-product-compliance
Lightning Source LLC
Chambersburg PA
CBHW071223050326
40689CB00011B/2426